Bread For The Journey

A High-Carb, Multisensory
Lenten Worship Series

Rolf Svanoe

CSS Publishing Company, Inc., Lima, Ohio

BREAD FOR THE JOURNEY

Library of Congress Cataloging-in-Publication Data

Svanoe, Rolf.
    Bread for the journey : a high-carb, multisensory Lenten worship series / Rolf Svanoe.
        p. cm.
    ISBN 0-7880-2507-4 (perfect bound : alk. paper)
    1. Lent—Meditations. 2. Cookery (Bread). 3. Children's sermons. I. Title.
    BV85.S83 2008
    242'.34—dc22

                                                                        2007040086

For more information about CSS Publishing Company resources, visit our website at
www.csspub.com or email us at csr@csspub.com or call (800) 241-4056.

Cover design by Barbara Spencer
ISBN-13: 978-0-7880-2507-5
ISBN-10: 0-7880-2507-4   PRINTED IN USA

To my colleagues and congregation at
Peace Lutheran Church,
Sioux Falls, South Dakota

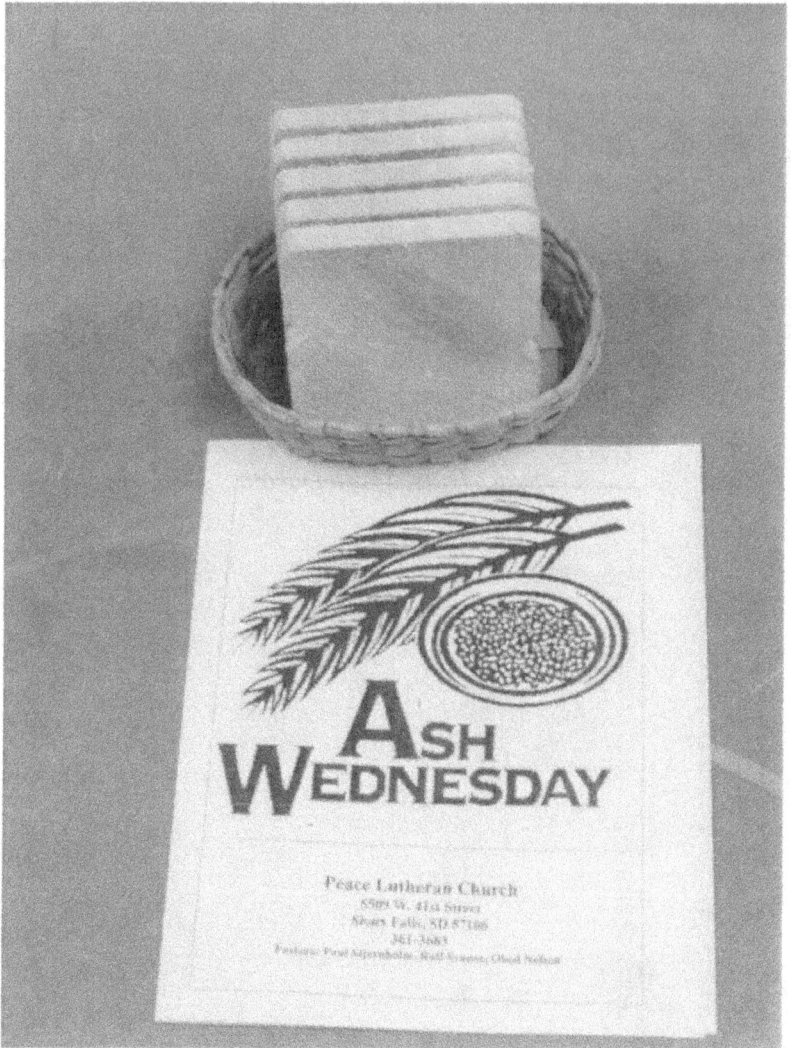

ASH
WEDNESDAY

Peace Lutheran Church
5505 W. 41st Street
Sioux Falls, SD 57106
361-3683
Pastors: Paul Aspenholm, Wall Svanoe, Obed Nelson

"I am the bread of life."

— Jesus

Table Of Contents

Introduction

Some of the most powerful memories are associated with the sense of smell. Get ready to create some powerful memories in your congregation as you lead them through this multisensory worship series: *Bread for the Journey.*

Bread is present throughout the pages of the Bible, but especially at key times of salvation history. These sermons and worship ideas give an opportunity to reflect on those stories in ways that are particularly appropriate for Lent, from Ash Wednesday all the way to Easter. Themes of hospitality, generosity, sufficiency, and trust are like slices in the loaf of bread being served each week.

D. T. Niles defined a Christian witness as one beggar who tells another beggar where to find bread. I think that's also a good definition of preaching. When hungry preachers feast on the bread of life and then share that bread with their congregations, they will be fed richly.

Many of the stories in the following sermons are personal. My hope is that they will help the preacher reflect on his/her experience and memories of bread. Share your own stories with your congregation. Be creative with the worship ideas in this book. I would love to hear how you have adapted and expanded them to your own setting.

These series grew out of my experience at three different congregations. I am indebted to colleagues and staff whose ideas have enriched and enhanced our worship far beyond what I originally envisioned. Thanks also to the editor at CSS who supplied many wonderful bread recipes. Finally, thanks to my wife, Kimberly, who was a most helpful reader of the manuscript.

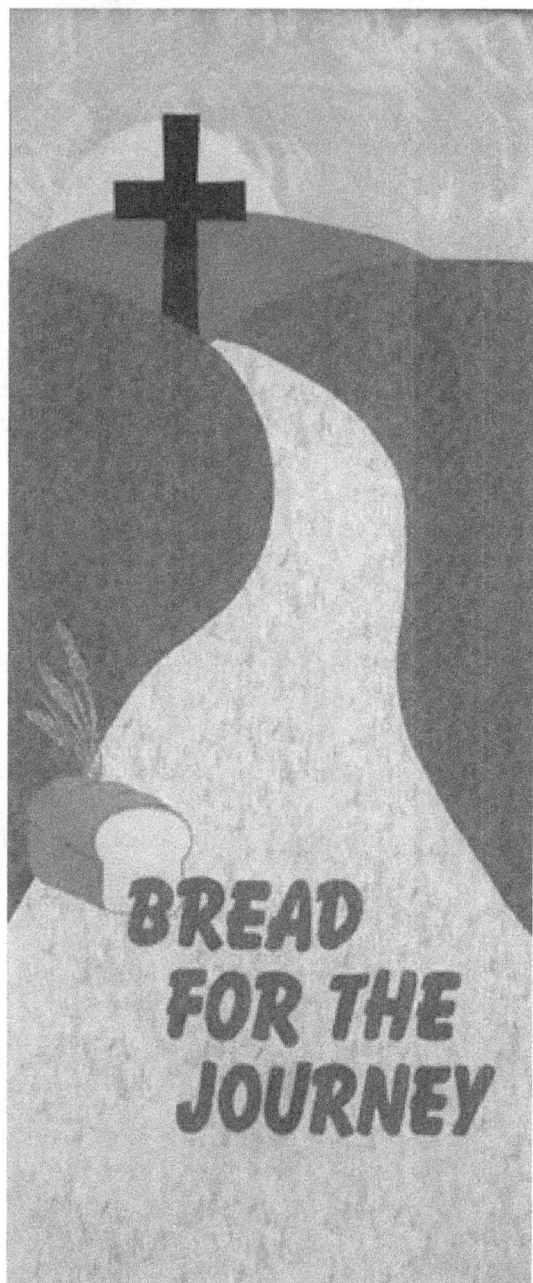

Banner design by Gwen Bobbie

Ways To Use This Series

Bake Bread

There is nothing better than the smell of fresh baked bread. So do it! Fill the sanctuary with the aroma of bread right out of the oven. Remember the bread machine craze a few years back? Ask your members to dust them off and bring them to church. Use the enclosed recipes, search the internet for bread machine recipes, or find out if your local grocery store sells bread mixes made for bread machines. If not, purchase them over the internet. Depending on the size of your sanctuary you might want to have two or three bread machines going. Spread them throughout the sanctuary so that wonderful smell gets everywhere. Time it so that the bread is done baking just before your service starts. Make sure to have one whole loaf to use for the children's sermon. Get ready for the deluge of children of all ages to come forward to get a piece of that delicious bread they can smell. Extra loaves can be cut into small pieces before the service. Let the children help distribute them to the congregation after the children's sermon so that everyone may have a taste.

Each week make a different kind of bread. Several recipes are included in these pages. Since Ash Wednesday and the services of Holy Week have so many traditions associated with them, some congregations may choose to serve bread only on the five mid-week services between them. The recipes have been included if you choose to bake for each service. There are additional recipes for those who wish to bake at additional services.

Children's Sermons

Children's messages are wonderful ways to include families in the service. Bake a different kind of bread each week and take some time to tell the children about the bread. For example, for Lent 2 make sourdough bread and explain how it is made from a starter. Use your imagination to make connections between the weekly theme and the bread recipe.

Lent 1: Welcome Bread — Honey Wheat Bread
Lent 2: Unleavened Bread — Sourdough Bread
Lent 3: Daily Bread — White Bread
Lent 4: More Than Bread — Exotic Bread
Lent 5: Abundant Bread — Barley Wheat Bread

Bread For The Journey Lenten Project

Why are happy meals at fast food restaurants so popular with kids? It's because they get a toy with the meal. And if there's a series of toys, children will drag their parents to the restaurant so they can collect every one of them. That's the idea behind a Lenten project.

Every year in our congregation we have a Lenten project, pieces that are handed out at each midweek service and collected by the congregation. Create an interesting project and they will want to collect them all. It's also a great way to involve volunteers. If you have a men's group in your church, put them to work using their woodworking skills. The Lenten project for *Bread for the Journey* is to hand out a small bread basket on Ash Wednesday. Mini wicker baskets in bulk quantities can be found inexpensively at your local craft store or over the internet. A small basket without a handle, about two inches by three inches is sufficient. The basket could have a piece of paper glued to the bottom that says something like "Bread for the Journey: Lent [Year]." Include your church name if you want. Each following week in Lent a small wooden slice of bread that fits in the basket will be given to the congregation. Your woodworkers can use their ingenuity to figure out how to make the appropriate size slice to fit the basket. Each slice of bread will have that week's theme on it. You can print the theme on adhesive labels and stick them on the slices. Another option is to have a rubber stamp company make the appropriate size stamp with the theme for each week. Include the scripture reference. Have volunteers stamp the pieces before handing them out to the congregation.

Midweek Worship

In many denominations, Ash Wednesday and the services of Holy Week have many valuable liturgical traditions, but the five midweek services between Ash Wednesday and Holy Week provide an opportunity for creative experimentation in worship. This series, in particular, encourages worship planners to open up all the senses, especially those of smell and taste.

Also provided is a theme song — "Bread For The Journey." The five verses reflect the five themes for midweek worship. You can add one verse each week or sing them all from the beginning as a foretaste of the themes to come. Finding appropriate hymns or contemporary songs to sing each week can be a challenge. Below you will find some suggestions of traditional hymns that could work.

Lent 1 — "O Living Bread From Heaven" (Aurelia)
Lent 2 — "When Israel Was In Egypt's Land" (Tubman)
Lent 3 — "Day By Day" (Blott En Dag)
Lent 4 — "Break Now The Bread Of Life" (Bread of Life)
Lent 5 — "Let Us Talents And Tongues Employ" (Linstead)

If your church has projection capability, that opens up a whole new area on which to focus. Put together a team to study the themes for each week and make suggestions for graphics to be included. Biblical images from classical artists are readily available on the internet. Check out websites like www.biblical-art.com or www.textweek.com (click on art index).

Lenten Dialogue

Leader:	Blessed are you, O Lord, our God, king of the universe.
Congregation:	**You bring forth bread from the earth.**
Leader:	Lord Jesus, you invite us this Lent to take up our cross and follow you.
Congregation:	**You promise that in losing our lives we will find them.**

Leader:	Help us to journey with you to the cross.
Congregation:	**Give us bread for our journey.**
Leader:	Jesus Christ is the bread of life; whoever eats of this bread will live forever.
Congregation:	**We feast on you, O Lord. You have the words of eternal life. Amen.**

Benediction

May the love of God, which gives life to the world, sustain you. May the bread of life, Jesus Christ, feed you with the food that endures to eternal life. May the power of the Holy Spirit nourish and strengthen you in faith. Amen.

Bread for the Journey

C G/B F/A G F9 Em7

Bread for the jour-ney, food for the way. Nour-ish - ing Spir - it

F/G C Am G F9 G

give bread to - day.

Wel - com - ing	stran-gers,	shar - ing	our	bread.
Yearn - ing	for free-dom,	slave - ry	to	cease;
Trust - ing	that dai - ly	God will	pro -	vide,
Bread with - out	Je - sus	can't sat -	is -	fy;
A - bun - dant	rich - es,	mir - a -	cle	food,

Am G/B Dm G

Christ in	our neigh - bor,	may all be	fed!
Bread of	de - liv'- rance,	God brings re -	lease.
Bread for	to - mor - row	won't be de -	nied.
Life's deep -	er mean - ing	God will sup -	ply.
Bread for	the hun - gry,	Je - sus is	good.

Bread for the Journey

Bread for the jour - ney, food for the way.

Nour - ish - ing Spir - it give bread to - day.

Wel - com - ing	stran - gers,	shar - ing	our	bread.
Yearn - ing	for free - dom,	slave - ry	to	cease;
Trust - ing	that dai - ly	God will	pro -	vide,
Bread with - out	Je - sus	can't sat -	is -	fy;
A - bun - dant	rich - es,	mir - a -	cle	food,

Christ in	our neigh - bor,	may all	be	fed!
Bread of	de - liv' - rance,	God brings	re -	lease.
Bread for	to - mor - row	won't be	de -	nied.
Life's deep - er	mean - ing	God will	sup -	ply.
Bread for	the hun - gry,	Je - sus	is	good.

Bread For The Journey

Some of the best memories I have as a child are associated with the sense of smell. I grew up living a block away from my grandparents and loved a certain cookie that Grandma would bake. Whenever I taste and smell those cookies today, the memories come flooding back. About a mile from our house was the Gardner Baking Company, and if the wind was just right, you could smell the bread baking in their ovens. It was delicious. Many children today do not have memories like that. We don't do as much baking in our homes today. This is one of the simple pleasures in life — the smell of fresh baked bread. Cutting a slice of hot bread and smothering it with butter and honey — it just doesn't get any better than that.

I met Tulla just after I arrived at my internship church. It was a wonderful church that took its role of training future pastors seriously. Tulla was an eighty-year-old widow of sturdy Danish stock. Being a young single man, she assumed that I really didn't know how to take care of myself; so she offered to wash my clothes for me. I didn't have the heart to refuse her. When she delivered my clothes, in the clothesbasket would be a couple loaves of homemade bread. Her bread was so delicious that after a few months I asked her to teach me how to make it. I became good at baking bread and I experimented with different recipes.

In former times, bread was not just a part of the meal. It *was* the meal. We're not talking about the kinds of processed bread you can buy today, but the kind of bread you sink your teeth into, that gives your jaw some exercise when you chew it. Substantial bread gives strength for a day's labor. This kind of bread was called the "staff of life," something to support and sustain us on our journey through life.

That's the kind of bread we have in our reading from Genesis 3:19. "By the sweat of your face you shall eat bread until you return to the ground, for out of it you were taken; you are dust, and to dust you shall return." We are on a journey, from dust to dust. God formed Adam and Eve from the dust of the ground. They died and returned to the dust of the ground. In between, it was the bread they ate that sustained them. And it sustains us. We live and love, we work and labor, we sweat to earn the money to put bread on our tables — bread for the journey, from dust to dust.

During these forty days of Lent, we are on a journey to the cross with Jesus. Our theme is "Bread for the Journey." We will eat bread, and we will be fed the Bread of Life. We will look at what the Bible has to say about bread and see how bread was present at the most significant events of the Old and New Testaments. Bread was there at the beginning when Adam and Eve fell into sin. God cursed them and said to them, "By the sweat of your face you shall eat bread until you return to the ground, for out of it you were taken; you are dust, and to dust you shall return." Adam and Eve's sin is our sin that we confess this night. It is our "age old rebellion," the desire to be God, to be in control and in charge, to decide for ourselves our future and what is right and wrong, to have no other masters telling us what to do.

Tonight we confess that we are not in charge, that we are not gods in control of our own destiny. We are dust, and to dust we shall return. We are reminded of that tonight, and we are reminded of that each time we stand at a graveside and hear those words, "earth to earth, ashes to ashes, dust to dust." We are creation, not creator. We are in bondage to sin, in need of a Savior. We look at the world around us and see the impact of sin — war and disease, hatred and violence, hunger and poverty, broken relationships and broken homes, people struggling with addictions and lifelong dysfunction. On this day we cannot wink at sin or laugh it off. Tonight we come to the cross with all our sinfulness. We return to the Lord with all our hearts.

Bread is a symbol of our lives. It has a journey of its own. It begins as a stalk of wheat, which at harvest time is *cut down*, its berries *ripped* from the stalk. The grain is *crushed* and *ground* together at the mill. The baker *mixes* and *kneads* and *punches* the dough. It's *thrown* into a hot oven and *baked*. These are words of violence and death, and yet through this process, wheat is transformed into something that gives life, nourishment, and strength to our bodies. Bread is a symbol of our lives. Its story is our story. We are never far from the experience of death. Its power touches our lives. Sometimes life cuts us down, rips us apart, and crushes us. But God is able to take whatever experience we have and make it into something new, like bread, something that gives us strength and hope and new life.

That is what God has done for us in Jesus Christ. The Bread of Life is the body of Christ, "wounded for our transgressions, crushed for our iniquities" (Isaiah 53:5). God took the evil and violence of the cross and transformed it into something that gives life, strength, and hope for the world. In Christ's death and resurrection, we are now offered the Bread of Life. It is bread for the journey, bread for this life and for all eternity. Thanks be to God.

"Whatever" Bread

Use whatever you find in the grab bag when making this recipe.

Ingredients
1 1/2 cups high-gluten bread flour
1 1/2 cups unbleached flour
1/2 cup wheat flour
1 Tablespoon olive oil
1 Tablespoon butter
2-3 Tablespoons honey or molasses
1 1/2 teaspoons sea salt
2 Tablespoons powdered milk
2 teaspoons yeast
1 large handful oat bran
1 handful raw sunflower seeds
1 handful raw pumpkin seeds
1 1/4 - 1 1/3 cups liquid (water or juice)

Directions
Add some seven-grain cereal, sesame seeds, flax seeds, or "whatever."

Throw the mixture into a bread machine and bake on regular cycle for wheat bread with a light crust.

Welcome Bread

When I was a college junior, a music group I played in took a trip to Europe. It was my first trip overseas and my first experience with another culture. My little world quickly became much bigger. One of our stops was in Stuttgart, Germany, home of the Mercedes-Benz Company. We stayed there for three days with host families. I remember the last night of our stay, our host lamented that we were leaving so soon. "You must come back again," he said to us. "Give me a few weeks notice and I'll take some vacation time. We'll travel to Switzerland to see the mountains." I remember being totally amazed at this gracious offer of hospitality. Why would this man make such a generous offer for strangers? Since then I have learned that showing remarkable hospitality is a custom in many countries. Indeed, some cultures are known for their hospitality.

Hospitality is one of the great themes of the Bible. In our reading, Abraham and Sarah welcomed three strangers to their tent. They were practicing the ancient law of the desert, which required that if a stranger appeared at your tent, you were to welcome them and give them food, drink, and shelter. It was a matter of survival that people depended on as they traveled in the desert. To welcome someone into your tent meant that you provided them not only with food and water, but also protection. Sharing food was a token of friendship, a covenant of commitment. To refuse to offer hospitality was seen as a hostile act, an affront that could lead to violence. But that wasn't why you welcomed strangers. And, you didn't do it for what you would get in return. You did it to protect your honor and reputation, and because someday you might be a stranger in need of help yourself.

Abraham and Sarah were gracious hosts, well-versed in the customs of hospitality. Notice how they attended to the needs of their guests.

19

The Lord appeared to Abraham by the oaks of Mamre,
as he sat at the entrance of his tent in the heat of the
day. He looked up and saw three men standing near
him. When he saw them, he ran from the tent entrance
to meet them, and bowed down to the ground. He said,
"My lord, if I find favor with you, do not pass by your
servant. Let a little water be brought, and wash your
feet, and rest yourselves under the tree. Let me bring a
little bread, that you may refresh yourselves, and after
that you may pass on — since you have come to your
servant." So they said, "Do as you have said." And
Abraham hastened into the tent to Sarah, and said,
"Make ready quickly three measures of choice flour,
knead it, and make cakes." Abraham ran to the herd,
and took a calf, tender and good, and gave it to the
servant, who hastened to prepare it. Then he took curds
and milk and the calf that he had prepared, and set it
before them; and he stood by them under the tree while
they ate ... Then the men set out from there, and they
looked toward Sodom; and Abraham went with them to
set them on their way. — Genesis 18:1-8, 16

Abraham begged these strangers to stay and give him an opportunity to serve them. He made them comfortable, providing them
water to wash with and a place to relax. He fed them meat and
bread — bread to sustain them for the rest of their journey. Good
hosts always look to the needs of the guest before their own, and
find joy in being able to meet their needs. When his guests left,
Abraham accompanied them to make sure they could find their
way.

Abraham and Sarah were just doing what was customary and
expected. Nothing in the story tells us that Abraham knew the special nature of the guests he was entertaining. But, in being faithful,
Abraham and Sarah received a blessing from God. Let's listen in
on the conversation that took place during the meal.

They said to him, "Where is your wife Sarah?" And he
said, "There, in the tent." Then one said, "I will surely
return to you in due season, and your wife Sarah shall

have a son." And Sarah was listening at the tent en-
trance behind him. Now Abraham and Sarah were old,
advanced in age; it had ceased to be with Sarah after
the manner of women. So Sarah laughed to herself,
saying, "After I have grown old, and my husband is
old, shall I have pleasure?" The Lord said to Abraham,
"Why did Sarah laugh, and say, 'Shall I indeed bear a
child, now that I am old?' Is anything too wonderful
for the Lord? At the set time I will return to you, in due
season, and Sarah shall have a son." But Sarah denied,
saying, "I did not laugh"; for she was afraid. He said,
"Oh yes, you did laugh."   — Genesis 18:9-15

It was an ordinary meal, sharing bread with strangers, extend-
ing hospitality and kindness. And yet, in being faithful, Abraham
and Sarah received a blessing that changed their lives forever —
the promise of a son. Having children was something for which
they had stopped hoping. The news that Sarah would have a son
was met with laughter and scorn. Little did they know that the guests
they had entertained spoke with God's voice and power. Is anything too wonderful for the Lord?

How many times have you failed to recognize God's presence
in your midst? Perhaps this story is behind that wonderful verse in
Hebrews: "Do not neglect to show hospitality to strangers, for by
doing that some have entertained angels without knowing it" (Hebrews 13:2). Do you recognize when God visits? Have you missed
a blessing God wants to give because you have neglected the
stranger among you?

It is clear that showing hospitality is one of the core teachings
of Jesus. "... for I was hungry and you gave me food, I was thirsty
and you gave me something to drink, I was a stranger and you
welcomed me ... Truly I tell you, just as you did it to one of the
least of these who are members of my family, you did it to me"
(Matthew 25:35, 40). Like Abraham and Sarah, when we share our
bread with the stranger in need, we are giving directly to God.

In one of his Christmas sermons, Martin Luther was preaching
to his congregation about the poor hospitality shown to Joseph and
Mary by the people of Bethlehem. "There are many of you who

21

think to yourselves: 'If only I had been there! How quick I would have been to help the baby!' ... You say that because you know how great Christ is, but if you had been there at that time you would have done no better than the people of Bethlehem ... Why don't you do it now? You have Christ in your neighbor."[1]

The person who has taught me the most about hospitality is the director of The Banquet, an ecumenical ministry in our city that provides a hot meal every day of the year to people who need help. Twice a year, our church prepares the food at The Banquet, and our confirmation students and parents serve it to 300-400 people. Before the doors are opened, the director meets with us and we read scripture and pray. She tells us that hospitality is an attitude of the heart. Giving hospitality requires that we overcome our fear of those who are strange to us and see Christ in them. Genuine hospitality means suspending judgments about the people we are serving, and creating a welcome space into which strangers can come and find themselves at home. On cold, winter nights, people are greeted at the door with a cup of hot cider or hot chocolate. Everyone is welcomed and treated with respect. Those who are there to serve are required to take a break from serving in order to eat and interact with the guests. Often students say that those conversations are the most meaningful part of the evening for them.

Tonight, Jesus invites us to share our bread. The amazing thing is that instead of being the host, we find that we are actually the guest, and that in sharing bread with others, Christ, the true host, is present to bring blessing into our lives. We are all strangers who have been graciously welcomed and made to feel at home. We are fed the family meal, the bread of life — Jesus Christ. Thanks be to God!

---

1. Martin Luther, *Martin Luther's Christmas Book*, Roland Bainton, editor (Minneapolis: Augsburg Fortress Publishers, 1997), p. 38.

Welcome Bread
(Honey Wheat)

(Your recipe this week should be a delicious bread — perhaps a honey wheat. Before this sermon, you will need to have your bread ready. Give some thought to how you want to distribute pieces of bread to the children. You can tear the loaf by hand or have pre-cut pieces ready to distribute. The children will need to help you carry pieces of bread to the congregation. Planners are encouraged to give thought as to how that process can best be accomplished. Perhaps three to four pieces of pre-cut bread cubes in a paper cup ready to go would be the easiest.)

Welcome, children. Did you smell something wonderful as you entered the sanctuary? Doesn't it smell good in here? Does it make your mouth water? I have some fresh baked bread here and I'm going to give you a piece of it so you can taste how wonderful it is. But before we do that let me tell you about this bread. We're going to call it "Welcome Bread."

Have you ever had guests or company come over to your home? What do your parents usually do when company comes? The first thing they do is to say, "Welcome! It's good to see you." We're glad to see our guests and we want to welcome them into our home. What else would Mom or Dad do for your guests? They might offer them something to eat or drink. In fact, you might all sit down to enjoy a meal together. That's what we often do with guests — share a meal together. We do that because we care about them. People get hungry and thirsty and we want to share our food and drinks with them.

We're going to hear some stories from the Bible where special guests arrived and shared a meal of bread. Abraham and Sarah had three guests arrive at their home and they hurried to welcome them with a meal that included bread. And you know, something amazing happened in that meal. Abraham and Sarah received a promise that they were going to have a baby. That made them very happy.

God asks us to share our bread. God does that because God loves us and gives us our daily bread. When we share our bread, we receive a blessing. It's amazing how that happens.

I'm going to share a piece of bread with you. *(give everyone a piece of bread)* Isn't that good? But we have a lot more bread to share and I need your help. Would you help me share this bread with everyone here tonight? When you take this bread to someone, I want you to say these words to them, "Welcome! God loves you." Can you do that? *(let them practice what they are to say a few times)* Wonderful. Before we do that, let us pray.

We thank you, Lord Jesus, that you love us and welcome us into your family. Thank you for this "welcome bread." Help us to share our bread and welcome each other. We love you, Jesus. Amen.

Honey Whole Wheat Bread

Ingredients
1 1/8 cups warm water (110 degrees F/45 degrees C)
3 Tablespoons honey
1/3 teaspoon salt
1 1/2 cups whole wheat flour
1 1/2 cups bread flour
2 Tablespoons canola or olive oil
1 1/2 teaspoons active dry yeast

Directions
Add ingredients according to the manufacturer's directions for the bread machine. Use the wheat bread cycle and light color setting.

Unleavened Bread

The other day, I picked up my daughter at high school and took her out for lunch. Our schools allow parents to do that if they call in advance. Since we didn't have much time, we decided to get fast food. While we were eating, she told me that in one of her classes that morning they had watched the film *Supersize Me*. It was part of a weeklong emphasis at school on healthy eating and the problems of obesity. For thirty days filmmaker Morgan Spurlock ate nothing but fast food from McDonald's — breakfast, lunch, and dinner. If he was asked whether or not he wanted his order supersized, he was obligated to say, "Yes" — hence the name of the film. During the month, he gained 25 pounds and his cholesterol jumped 60 points. His doctors were shocked by the negative impact of his diet, and two weeks into his experiment, they asked him to stop. My daughter told me all this while we were wolfing down our burgers and fries. "Sixty percent of Americans are obese," she said. "Sixty percent, can you believe that?" As we sat there in the restaurant, we had more than fast food to chew on. I suggested that perhaps we should give up fast food for Lent. She made me pinky swear.

Jay Leno, on *The Tonight Show*, likes to poke fun at how fat Americans are getting. It's true that fast food in America contributes to this problem. This Lent, I invite you to eat a different kind of fast food, one found in the Bible. In our reading from Exodus, we have the original fast food. God's people were enslaved in Egypt and they cried out to God to deliver them. God heard their prayers and used a series of plagues to change the mind of their oppressors. Before the last plague, God commanded his people to eat a special meal. They were to kill a sheep or goat, put its blood on the doorposts, roast it, and eat it with bitter herbs and unleavened bread. "This is how you shall eat it: your loins girded, your sandals on your feet, and your staff in your hand; and you shall eat it hurriedly. It is the passover of the Lord" (Exodus 12:11). Another translation puts it this way, "... you are to eat it quickly, for you are to be dressed for travel ..." (Exodus 12:11 TEV). Fast food! God was about to deliver them. The angel of death would pass over the homes marked with lamb's blood, but visit the other homes with the death of the firstborn. A drastic measure was needed to free God's people from their oppressors. And, when it happened, they needed to be ready to go.

Have you ever eaten matzah? *Matzah* is the Hebrew word for unleavened bread. You can buy it in most grocery stores in the ethnic foods section. It's a flat bread that when baked has the look of a cracker. The bread is flat because it is made quickly without yeast. Proper bread takes time to rise. Yeast works in the dough producing gas, which over time will cause the dough to expand. But the Passover meal was to be different. There was no time to allow the bread to rise. God's people were in a hurry. God was about to rescue them. They didn't have the time for a leisurely meal. They needed to be ready to travel.

But there was another reason for the unleavened bread. It symbolized a break from the past. People would use a pot of starter to make their bread, a piece of fermented dough from the bread made the day before. They would add it to the new dough they were mixing so it would ferment. A piece of that new fermented dough would then be stored away and used as starter for the next loaf of bread. By making unleavened bread, God's people were concretely demonstrating their break from the past. It wasn't just bread starter they left behind. They had lived in Egypt for hundreds of years and had learned Egyptian language, culture, and religion. God wanted them to have a complete break with Egypt in every way. If God was going to create a new people with new laws, they needed a clean break from their past.

Leaving Egypt behind was something so important that God commanded it to be remembered every year, passed on from generation to generation.

Unleavened bread shall be eaten for seven days; no leavened bread shall be seen in your possession, and no leaven shall be seen among you in all your territory. You shall tell your child on that day, "It is because of what the Lord did for me when I came out of Egypt." It shall serve for you as a sign on your hand and as a reminder on your forehead, so that the teaching of the Lord may be on your lips; for with a strong hand the Lord brought you out of Egypt. You shall keep this ordinance at its proper time from year to year.
— Exodus 13:7-10

Leaving Egypt behind was something every generation needed to do.

There is a huge difference between leavened and unleavened bread. Leavened bread is the bread of those who are comfortable and settled, those with homes and kitchens with ovens. These are the people with time to let bread rise, to let Emeril Lagasse teach us how to "kick it up a notch," or Martha Stewart show us how to set a beautiful table. But matzah, unleavened bread, is the "bread of affliction," the bread of those in turmoil and transition, the bread of those in need of rescue and deliverance. Matzah is the bread of those who need changes in their lives because life isn't working. Matzah is for all who yearn for freedom.

Like matzah, Lent is a season of the church year that unsettles us. We are not in bondage to Egyptian oppressors, but we are indeed slaves. Jesus said, "Everyone who commits sin is a slave to sin" (John 8:34). In our liturgy we confess that "we are in bondage to sin and cannot free ourselves." Lent is the season that will not leave us settled, comfortable, or well-fed. It reminds us of our daily struggle against sin and temptation. Prayer, repentance, fasting, and charity are the disciplines of Lent. They are the marks of those who look to God for deliverance from the power of sin.

Lent calls us to leave Egypt behind and look to Christ alone. God's people are called to be "in the world" but not "of the world" (John 17). We are called to live counter "to" culture, resisting the seductive invitations to live for self alone. Wealth, power, and pleasure are the gods we are called to leave behind today, to reject the

29

lie that these gods will give us happiness, joy, or peace. We are called to follow Christ and find that in relationship with him we find abundant life, joy, and peace beyond anything the world can give.

The Passover meal included both unleavened bread and roasted lamb. It was the lamb's blood that saved the Israelites from the angel of death. Today it is the blood of the Lamb of God, Jesus Christ, that takes away the sin of the world and saves us from death (John 1:29). Have you ever wondered why in Holy Communion we eat those thin wafers? They don't look or taste much like bread. It comes from the tradition of using unleavened bread. Not all churches follow that custom, but I think it is a helpful one. Unleavened bread is the original fast food for people ready to travel, yearning for freedom. But this fast food won't clog your arteries or raise your cholesterol. It heals our hearts and brings new life. Today, Christ comes to us in bread and wine to forgive our sins and give us a foretaste of freedom. Thanks be to God.

Unleavened Bread
(Sourdough Bread)

(This week you will need to purchase or bake some matzah bread to show the children what unleavened bread looks like. The bread recipe this week is sourdough. Again, you may want to have pre-cut pieces so the children can eat the bread and share it easily with the congregation.)

Welcome, children. Good to see you again. Tonight I have two kinds of bread to show you. The first is called sourdough bread and I'd like to share a piece with you. Tastes a little tangy, doesn't it? People have made sourdough bread for thousands of years. The dough is made from a starter. You add it to your bread mixture and the starter helps the bread to start rising. You save a little bit of your mixture so you can use it as the starter for the next batch of bread you bake. That's how you make sourdough bread.

Have you ever seen bread like this before? *(Show them the matzah. You may want to give them each a piece to taste.)* It looks like a cracker, doesn't it? It's called matzah and it's a special bread made without starter. That's why it stays flat. There is a wonderful story in the Bible about matzah bread. It's a story during the time of Moses when God's people were in Egypt. Life was very hard for those people and God promised that he would come and rescue them. They were supposed to make bread without a starter because God wanted them to be ready to leave Egypt. They couldn't wait around for the bread to rise. God's people had to be ready to go.

Tonight we have freedom bread. It is the bread God gives us to remind us that God wants us to be free. That's why God sent Jesus to us, so that we could be free.

Can you help me share this bread with the congregation? When you give someone a piece of bread, I want you to say, "Jesus says you are free!" Can you say that with me? *(let them repeat it a few times)* Very good. Now, let us pray.

Lord Jesus, thank you for freedom bread and the reminder that you love us so much that you free us to follow you. Bless these children throughout this week. Amen.

Unleavened Bread

Before you start mixing all ingredients, turn oven on and pre-heat to 425 degrees F.

Ingredients
2 cups of flour (increase all ingredients for larger recipe)
3/4 cup liquid (try kosher wine and water mixed)
1/2 cup oil (olive is the best)
1 cup sugar

Directions
Mix together. Divide into pieces and flatten. Adjust liquid if needed. Pierce each cake with a fork. Bake until edges are brown, about fifteen minutes.

Sourdough Bread

Ingredients
1 cup warm water
1 Tablespoon sugar
1 teaspoon salt
2 Tablespoons oil
4 cups flour
1 1/2 cups sourdough starter
1 package active dry yeast

Directions
Put all ingredients into bread machine in the order listed. Select the basic setting and change the crust setting to light.

Sourdough Bread Starter

Ingredients
1 Tablespoon yeast
2 cups bottled water (or well water)
2 cup unbleached white flour

Directions
Mix all ingredients together in a nonmetal container (an earthenware container works well), cover lightly with plastic wrap, and leave alone in a warm place (70-75 degrees F) for two to three days. It'll start foaming and have a sour (although not offensive) yeasty smell.

At this point, move the starter to the refrigerator. It needs to be fed twice a week, to keep it growing. Feed it by using or discarding two cups of the starter, then add 1 1/2 cups flour and 1 1/2 cups water to the original bowl. Stir, cover, and return to the refrigerator. You can use it after it's a few days old, though it will develop a more "sourdoughish" flavor after a few weeks. If it turns odd colors or starts growing mold, discard it and start over. If your starter fails to "start" (it doesn't foam or bubble), try a different brand or batch of yeast.

Lent 3
Exodus 16:1-21; Luke 11:1-4

Daily Bread

A few years ago, a young American man was lost in the Australian desert. Robert Bogucki, a 33-year-old volunteer fireman from Fairbanks, Alaska, was on vacation in Australia. Robert did some sightseeing and then headed off across the Australian desert "seeking spiritual enlightenment." The young man was missing something in his life, and he felt that in the wilderness of Australia he could discover something about himself and about God. After two weeks, his absence sparked an intensive search that ended with his discovery. He had spent some forty days in the wilderness. Robert kept himself alive eating plants and wildflowers and drinking dirty water. In forty days, he lost 44 pounds. A television crew flying in a helicopter just happened to spot him. On the hour-long flight back to civilization, Robert was asked why he had embarked on the journey. "I just wanted to spend a while on my own, just nobody else around, just make peace with God, I guess," he said. Robert said he felt alone in the desert but never believed he was going to die, even when his supplies ran out. "I had the feeling of confidence that God would take care of me," he said.[1]

This searching to find oneself in the desert, in a tough, austere environment, alone, away from the comforts of everyday life, is not uncommon in many cultures. In some Native American cultures there is a rite-of-passage ritual into adulthood called the Vision Quest in which a young man leaves home and undergoes a period of testing and denial in order to discover who he is and what his place is in the community. Many people today refer to the desert or wilderness as a spiritual place. I think of it as a place where distractions are left behind. It's a place to focus on things that often lie hidden below the surface of our lives waiting for some day when we will pay attention to them.

After God rescued the Israelites from their slavery in Egypt, Moses led them into the wilderness, heading toward Mount Sinai. It was time to learn some important lessons about this God who had rescued them, and what better place than in the wilderness. But the Israelites didn't like the wilderness. They began to complain. "I'd rather die a slave in Egypt than die of hunger and thirst out here in this godforsaken wilderness. Life may not have been good in Egypt, but at least we had something to eat." It's interesting how the story continues. It doesn't say that God was angry at them or that God scolded them for their ingratitude. It just says that God decided to provide for them. Every morning, the people could go out and collect bread. It was a flaky substance they called manna. In Hebrew, the word *manna* literally translates, "What is it?" They looked at this strange food and said, "What is this stuff?"

You know, it seems like we eat a lot of manna at our house. Every time I make something different to eat, my kids look at it with suspicion and say, "Oo — what is that?" I like to reply, "We're having manna tonight. It is the food your Lord is providing you." Why are children so reluctant to taste something new? They want the old and familiar. Maybe there's a reason why the Bible refers to the Israelites as the "children" of Israel.

So God provided the Israelites with manna bread, and with the manna came a test. They were to gather each morning only enough to meet their needs for that day. If they gathered more than they needed, if they tried to store it or hoard it, the manna spoiled — it turned rotten and became worm-infested. The basic issue was whether there was going to be something to eat the next day or not. This was the lesson they were to learn in the wilderness — to trust God to provide for each day. And when they trusted that God would provide, God was found to be faithful. Manna came each day. They didn't need to worry about whether or not they had food to eat.

It seems to me that we can learn a lot today from these ancient lessons in the wilderness. **First: Trust God to provide for your future.** As the Israelites gathered manna every day, and they experienced God's faithfulness, they began to trust that God would provide for the future. They didn't need to worry whether the manna would be there tomorrow or not. They didn't need to hoard it because they felt insecure about the future. What about us? Do we trust God to provide for our future needs? Or do we save and hoard what we have so that we can have a secure future? I'm not smart enough to figure out what this lesson might have to say about our savings accounts, our pension plans, our 401Ks, and IRAs. There is a lot of wisdom in setting aside now to be able to enjoy security in the future. The question is where we put our trust. Do we put more trust in our investments than we put in God? One of the ways the Bible encourages us to answer that question is by giving away a portion of our income. It's called the tithe. Instead of saving for our future, we give some money away now trusting that God will faithfully provide for our future as we faithfully give to him today. Now we could keep that money for ourselves. We could find lots of reasons why we can't afford to give, but the lesson of the wilderness is that if we trust only in our wealth and hoard it, we will find that in the end our wealth has spoiled and become worm-infested. God doesn't give us today what we will need for tomorrow because he wants us to trust him. And God wants us to be faithful with what he's given us today. That's the first lesson — Trust God to provide for your future.

There is a second lesson we can learn from the wilderness: **God will meet your need, not your greed.** God didn't give the Israelites what they wanted; he gave them what they needed. He didn't provide them with T-bone steak. He gave them something basic — bread, manna. They may not have liked the manna. They may have complained about it, but at least God met their basic need for food. God met their need, not their greed.

Have you ever been to a "parade of homes"? The homes on display are usually expensive. It's fun to look through them and imagine yourself living there. But it's dangerous, too. I find myself leaving with a feeling of dissatisfaction. I look at my car, my house, and my tired and worn possessions. Wouldn't it be nice to have a newer model car, a bigger house, a faster computer, more clothes, more whatever? You fill in the blank. We all have those things in our life that we desire, and the lie is that owning these things will make us happier. The reality is that if we follow our desires we will never have enough; we will always end up wanting more.

In the Lord's Prayer, Jesus taught us to pray for daily bread. He, too, had learned the lessons of the wilderness. But Jesus added a lesson of his own. Our prayer for daily bread is always prayed in community. We don't ask for my daily bread. Bread is not mine alone. Bread is given by God for the community. Daily bread is meant to be shared. In the Lord's Prayer, we pray that the whole world may be fed. This idea is expressed well in a poem that someone sent me.

> *You cannot pray the Lord's Prayer and even once say "I."*
> *You cannot pray the Lord's Prayer and even once say "My."*
> *Nor can you pray the Lord's Prayer and not pray for one another,*
> *And when you ask for daily bread, you must include your brother.*
> *For others are included in each and every plea,*
> *From the beginning to the end of it, it does not once say "Me."*[2]

The lesson of the wilderness is that God promises to meet our needs. Jesus knows that our most basic need in life is for a relationship with him, a relationship where we find forgiveness for our sins and an unconditional love and grace. Jesus offers you that today. Thanks be to God.

---

1. Associated Press, *World: Asia-Pacific American Found After Outback Odyssey*, BBC News, August 23, 1999. http://news.bbc.co.uk/2/hi/asia-pacific/428505.stm (accessed June 24, 2007).

2. From the Omaha Home for Boys, 4343 N. 52nd Street, Omaha, Nebraska 68104.

Daily Bread
(Favorite White Bread)

Welcome, children. I'm glad you're here this evening because I have another kind of bread to share with you. This is a basic white bread, the kind of bread you might have for breakfast or lunch. *(pass out pieces for the children to taste)* It tastes good, doesn't it? But it might taste even better if we put something on it. Do any of you eat toast for breakfast? What do you like to put on your toast? What about lunch — do you eat sandwiches? What's your favorite thing to put on a sandwich? It's hard to beat peanut butter and jelly, isn't it?

Many people eat bread every day. I imagine some of you eat bread every day. Do you ever run out of bread at your house? What do you do? It's easy to go to the grocery store and buy a loaf of bread. Maybe some of you make bread at your house.

I want to tell you a story from the Bible about how God provided God's people with bread. It was a special kind of bread called manna. It wasn't anything fancy — just basic bread. And God gave it to God's people every day. It was daily bread. They became hungry and God fed them because God loved them.

Jesus taught us to pray for daily bread. He said when we pray we should say, "Give us this day our daily bread." God wants us to trust every day that God will provide for our needs. And God does that for us because God loves us. God loves you. That's why when we eat a meal, we usually say a prayer to thank God for our food.

Can you help me share this bread with the congregation again? When you give each person a piece of bread, I want you to say the words, "God gives you daily bread." Please say that with me. *(let them repeat it a few times)*

41

Let us pray together. Thank you, God, for daily bread. Thank you that you love us so much that you provide for our daily needs. Help us to be aware of those who are hungry and to share our bread with them. We love you, Jesus. Amen.

White Bread

Ingredients
4 teaspoons of active yeast
1 1/3 cups warm water
4 cups white flour
1 Tablespoon milk power
2 teaspoons sugar
1 teaspoon salt
2 Tablespoons melted margarine

Directions

Put first two ingredients into bread pan. Mix around and let stand in a warm place until yeast starts to work, then add the remainder of the ingredients.

Put the pan into the machine. Bake on French bake, with a light crust or as per manual.

Makes a high rise loaf.

Sweet White Bread

Ingredients
1 cup water (80 degrees F/27 degrees C)
2 Tablespoons oil
1/2 cup sugar
1 1/4 teaspoons salt
1 1/2 Tablespoons evaporated milk
2 1/2 cups flour
2 teaspoons (1 pkg.) active dry yeast

Directions
Add ingredients to the bread machine in the above order. Use the regular setting, with medium crust.

This recipe yields 1 1/2-pound loaf. It is a very sweet white bread — delicious!

More Than Bread

Some of my earliest memories from childhood are of times when our family gathered to eat. The table was set and the food was prepared. Mom had an old cowbell that she used to ring outside. You could hear it a block away. Wherever we were playing, we knew it was time to come home for supper when we heard that bell. We washed our hands and sat down at the table, all eight of us. The first thing we did was to pray. Usually, we sang. We had several different songs we used as table prayers — "God is great and God is good," "Come and dine, the Master calleth, come and dine," and "Praise God from whom all blessings flow." We even had to learn a prayer in Norwegian. Only after we said our prayers could we eat. I don't remember how all eight of us fit around the table. What I do remember is what happened after the meal. We got out our Bibles and read through a chapter. I remember sitting there so impatiently, wanting to get outside and play with my friends. But it was important, and so we did it, even with all the grumbling. We had fed the body, and now it was time to feed the soul. My parents were impressing two things on me at a tender age: It is God who provides our food, and food alone is not enough to give meaning to our lives.

It's so easy to forget that our food comes from God. In his explanation of the Lord's Prayer in his *Small Catechism*, Martin Luther said, "God gives daily bread, even without our prayer, to all people, though sinful, but we ask in this prayer that God will help us to realize this and receive our daily bread with thanks." We need help to realize this because we often forget that it really comes from God. We work hard, earn our money, buy food at the store, and take time to prepare it. Why should we thank God for it? The author of Deuteronomy tried to answer that question when he gave the Israelites a warning, just before they entered the promised land.

Take care that you do not forget the Lord your God, by failing to keep his commandments, his ordinances, and his statutes, which I am commanding you today. When you have eaten your fill and have built fine houses and live in them, and when your herds and flocks have multiplied, and your silver and gold is multiplied, and all that you have is multiplied, then do not exalt yourself, forgetting the Lord your God ... Do not say to yourself, "My power and the might of my own hand have gotten me this wealth." But remember the Lord your God, for it is he who gives you power to get wealth, so that he may confirm his covenant that he swore to your ancestors, as he is doing today. — Deuteronomy 8:11-18*

When you buy bread, what do you really pay for? You pay for the farmer and the seed and for the tractor, combine, and truck. You've paid for the storage time in the grain elevator and the mill that grinds the grain into flour. You've paid for the bakers and the ovens that baked the bread. You've paid for the truck driver who delivered it to the store. You've paid for the person to stock the bread shelves and the clerk to check it out. But what have you paid for the bread? Not one cent. It is God who gives bread. It is God who makes the wheat to grow. It is God who sustains our lives and gives us strength and creativity to work and earn money.[1]

There was another thing the author of Deuteronomy was concerned about. He was worried that in the new land the Israelites would forget God. They would settle into their homes, get rich, and be comfortable. They would be so busy making a living they would forget to make a life with God.

This entire commandment that I command you today you must diligently observe, so that you may live and increase, and go in and occupy the land that the Lord promised on oath to your ancestors. Remember the long way that the Lord your God has led you these forty years in the wilderness, in order to humble you, testing you to know what was in your heart, whether or not you would keep his commandments. He humbled you

46

by letting you hunger, then by feeding you with manna,
with which neither you nor your ancestors were ac-
quainted, in order to make you understand that one does
not live by bread alone, but by every word that comes
from the mouth of the Lord.   — Deuteronomy 8:1-3

That sermon was preached over 3,000 years ago. It was true then, and it's still true now. We don't live by bread alone. Living only to satisfy our physical needs will not make for a complete life. There are spiritual needs to satisfy, too. We have a God-shaped hole in our hearts that can only be filled by God. Don't forget God and God's word. Remember all the things God has done and is doing for you.

Jesus quoted these words when he faced temptation in the desert.

Then Jesus was led up by the Spirit into the wilderness
to be tempted by the devil. He fasted forty days and
forty nights, and afterwards he was famished. The
tempter came and said to him, "If you are the Son of
God, command these stones to become loaves of bread."
But he answered, "It is written, 'One does not live by
bread alone, but by every word that comes from the
mouth of God.' "   — Matthew 4:1-4

It's as if the devil was saying to Jesus, "Go ahead, Jesus, satisfy your desires and your hunger with things. Turn the stones to bread. It will satisfy you, and give purpose to your life."

Several years ago, a controversial movie came out called *The Last Temptation of Christ*. Based on a book by Nikos Kazantzakis, the movie was controversial because people did not understand the fictional story behind it. The fantasy takes place while Jesus is hanging on the cross. In a stupor, Jesus lives out a fantasy of getting down off the cross, forsaking his mission, and having a normal, quiet life. He does his carpentry work, he marries, and he has children. He discusses religion with his close friends, and he grows old. The end of this dream is that Jesus, as an old man, is confronted by his disciples, a bunch of decrepit, spiritless old men. In

47

a twist of irony, Judas accuses Jesus of having been a coward, a deserter, and a traitor for having come down from the cross. In Judas' opinion, Jesus had wasted his life by avoiding the cross where God had wanted him. He had chosen an easier way and become a failure. In a passage at the end of the book Jesus awoke from his dream, still hanging on the cross, and realized that he had faced his final temptation, a temptation to live for himself instead of following God.

> *Temptation had captured him for a split second and led him astray. The joys, marriages, and children were lies; the decrepit, degraded old men who shouted coward, deserter, traitor at him were lies. All — all were illusions sent by the Devil. His disciples were alive and thriving. They had gone over sea and land and were proclaiming the Good News. Everything had turned out as it should, glory be to God! He uttered a triumphant cry: "It is accomplished!" And it was as though he had said: "Everything has begun."[2]*

Let's be honest. Aren't there times when we want to avoid God's will for our lives? Who wants to take up a cross? Then there are times we doubt God's existence or love. Wouldn't it just be easier to stay home Sunday morning, have some family time, sleep in, take care of ourselves, catch up on reading, news, chores, or whatever? Wouldn't it be easier to spend all our time, energy, or money on ourselves and our families, to forget about the needs of others, and all the suffering in the world? Wouldn't it be easier to live without God, without Jesus, without the cross?

Saint Augustine said that the heart is restless until it rests in God. Moses and Jesus said one does not live by bread alone. We can live for the moment and try to fill our lives with all kinds of pleasures and things, but in the end, it is empty. We need something more than bread; we need the Bread of Life.

Jesus faced his temptation head on. He went to the cross. He gave his body as the bread of life for the world. Eating this bread brings forgiveness of sins and eternal life. Eating this bread brings hope and meaning to our daily lives. It gives us strength to face the temptation to live our lives without God.

----

1. Harry Wendt, *An Apostle's Creed for the New Millennium*, 2nd ed. (Minneapolis: Crossways International, 2004), p. 24.

2. Nikos Kazantzakis, *The Last Temptation of Christ*, trans. P. A. Bien (New York: Simon and Schuster, 1960), p. 496.

More Than Bread
(Your Favorite Exotic Bread —
Cinnamon Raisin)

Welcome, children. This week we have another bread to share. Let me give you a piece of bread and you tell me what it tastes like. Can you guess what it is? This is my favorite bread. In fact, I love it so much that I could live on it if it was the only food I had to eat. Do you think you'd get tired of eating bread if that's all you ever had to eat?

The Bible tells us that bread is a good gift from God. God gives us daily bread. God wants us to share our bread with others. Bread is important. But there is something more important than bread, something more important than food. Do you know what could possibly be more important than food for us? It is our relationship with God. Bread will only fill our tummies when we are hungry. But only God can fill our hearts. Jesus said that we can't live on bread alone. We need something more — we need God. When we read the Bible, or when we come to worship to hear the Bible read, God feeds us deep down, in our hearts. The Bible tells us that God loves us. When we are sad, God cries with us, and when we are happy, God laughs with us. That is something bread cannot do. That's why we need God. That's why we need Jesus.

Will you help me share our bread with the congregation? When you give away a piece of bread I want you to say these words, "More than bread, you need Jesus." Say that with me. *(let them repeat it a few times)* Thank you. You are all preachers tonight.

Let's say a prayer. Lord Jesus, we thank you for bread, but more than that, we thank you for you. Feed us with your bread of life. Feed our hearts with your word. Help us grow strong in loving you. Amen.

Buttermilk Cinnamon Raisin Bread

Ingredients
1 cup plus 2 Tablespoons buttermilk
3 Tablespoons butter, cut up into small pieces
1 teaspoon nutmeg
3 teaspoons cinnamon
3 Tablespoons sugar, preferably brown
1/2 teaspoon salt
2 1/2 cups bread flour
1/2 cup wheat flour
1 teaspoon bread machine yeast
3/4 cup raisins

Directions
Add ingredients to the bread machine as directed, except for raisins. Use light crust, regular setting, and check for dough consistency after five minutes. If your machine beeps for add-ins, add raisins then. If not, add them five minutes after the second kneading starts.

Notes
To keep raisins from sticking together, or "clumping," put the raisins in a baggie with 1 teaspoon bread flour and shake. This way, raisins will be throughout your bread. Do not use "baking raisins," as they will fall apart.

This bread is also good with 1/2 cup bits and pieces of walnuts or pecans, added when the raisins are added.

Also, try a powdered sugar icing — *very* good! Use 1 cup powdered sugar, 1 teaspoon vanilla, and add milk 1 teaspoon at a time while stirring. This needs to be fairly thick or will not harden at all. Drizzle the icing over mostly cooled bread and let icing run down sides. Enjoy!

Orange Almond Bread

Ingredients
2 cups bread flour
1 teaspoon baking powder
1/2 teaspoon baking soda
3/4 cup white sugar
3 Tablespoons vegetable oil
2 eggs
juice from two medium-sized oranges
3/4 cups crushed almonds
dried orange peel (from the spice rack)

Directions
Place ingredients (except the orange peel) in the pan of the bread machine.

Select the dough setting of sweet bread and press start. Let it cycle through the kneading.

Sprinkle the orange peel on the dough after the kneading cycle is done.

This recipe creates a crunchy crust, moist interior bread.

Abundant Bread

It was almost 35 years ago, but I can still see his face, staring into mine, pleading with me. I was seventeen years old working at a Sears store in Los Angeles. It was December and I had a temporary job selling Christmas trees in the garden department. My big excitement was unloading the trees from the truck. The trees were from Oregon and snow was still packed in their branches. It was the only time I saw snow in Los Angeles, and that was exciting to a boy who had grown up in the Midwest and who thought that Christmas wasn't real without snow. It was a busy evening, with lots of people looking for that special tree to decorate their homes. A man arrived. He looked to be in his seventies, and rather frail. Dressed in a black suit, there was a certain dignity about him. The clothes he wore must have been nice at one time, but now looked rather threadbare and worn. He was having a hard time communicating with another sales person. It was obvious he spoke little English. That's not so unusual in Los Angeles, with people there from all over the world. But my ears perked up as I caught his accent. German, I guessed. I was learning German in high school; so I wandered over to see if I could help.

As we talked, the man was relieved that here was someone who could understand him and he grabbed on to me as if I was an answer to his prayers. Quickly he explained his dilemma. He had no money. Times were hard. He lived with his daughter and grandchildren. There was no money left to celebrate Christmas. They had barely enough to buy food. It would make such a difference if they could have a tree. Would I help him? It was a pitiful story. He looked uncomfortable, obviously not used to asking for help. My heart was moved for him, but what could I do? I was just a salesperson expected to sell trees at the marked price. There was no room for me to barter and no authority for me to give trees away.

53

"I'm sorry," I told him. "There's nothing I can do." We went on like that for five minutes, with him trying to convince me to help him and me telling him I could not help him. Finally, in his most pleading voice, he clutched his arms to his breast and said, *"Hilf mir! Bitte, hilf mir!"* which means, "Help me! Please, help me!" And then, right there in the store, he got on his knees, clutched my legs, looked into my eyes, and said more pleadingly, *"Hilf mir!"* I was embarrassed by the scene that was created, but it was only then that a deeper truth dawned on me. I could help him. I was not defined by my role as an employee of Sears. I began to think outside that box. I was a human being that could respond to the desperate cry for help from another human being. *"Hilf mir!"* The words and the look in his eyes tugged at my heart, one human being to another. *"Hilf mir!"* Only the coldest heart could say, "No," to that kind of cry. Moved to compassion, I gave him enough money to buy a small tree that he could carry home with him.

The memory of his words and his face came back to me as I read this miracle story, multiplied 5,000 times. Huge crowds gathered around Jesus, longing to see and hear him. Some, having heard of the miracles Jesus had performed, were desperate for healing. It was as if they were on their collective knees crying out to Jesus, "Help me!" In the lesson, Mark says that Jesus felt great compassion for them and began to teach them. Usually, when faced with such numbers, it's tempting to give up. What can one person do for so many people? But not Jesus. Compassion demanded a response.

When it grew late, and everyone was tired and hungry, the disciples asked Jesus to send the crowds away to the surrounding villages to buy something to eat. They were being logical and practical. They didn't have enough food for such a crowd. They didn't even have enough money to buy food for them. They suggested to Jesus the only possible thing they could think of — dismiss the crowd to go find their own meals. But not Jesus. Compassion demanded a response. "You give them something to eat," Jesus said. The disciples must have thought he was crazy. There was no way they could find enough bread to feed a crowd of 5,000 people. Their options were as limited as their imaginations. But not Jesus. The disciples looked at five loaves of bread and two fish, and felt helpless. Jesus looked at the same bread and fish, and gave thanks. He blessed and broke the loaves of bread, and somehow everyone ate. And it wasn't just crumbs. Everyone ate their fill and there were leftovers!

I wonder if God's people aren't doing the same thing today the disciples did back then — thinking inside the box with limited imaginations when we are faced with human need. The numbers are staggering — 854 million people are hungry.[1] The problem is not that there isn't enough food. God has certainly blessed the world with enough to feed everyone on the planet. We know the problem is not supply, but distribution. The problem is wealthy nations lacking the political will to end poverty and hunger. The problem is too many people overwhelmed with the problem thinking inside the box with limited imaginations.

In a bold new book called *The End of Poverty*, Jeffrey D. Sachs discusses how we can make it happen. He is the director of the UN Millennium Project, which has the goal of helping to cut the world's extreme poverty in half by 2015. He outlines his proposals in his book. "We can banish extreme poverty in our generation — yet eight million people die each year because they are too poor to survive. The tragedy is that with a little help, they could even thrive."[2] His ideas center around the adoption of different economic practices that could feed the hungry.

The traditional disciplines of Lent are prayer, fasting, and acts of charity. Lent reminds us of the need to deny self and give to others, especially the poor and needy. It is time to learn the lessons of the miracle feeding of 5,000. God can use small things to work great miracles.

The apostle Paul learned these stewardship lessons. In his second letter to the church at Corinth he explained it this way:

> *And God is able to provide you with every blessing in abundance, so that by always having enough of every-thing, you may share abundantly in every good work ... He who supplies seed to the sower and bread for food will supply and multiply your seed for sowing and in-crease the harvest of your righteousness.*
> — 2 Corinthians 9:8, 10

"You give them something to eat." These were Jesus' words to his disciples back then, and they are still his words to his disciples today. In surrendering what little we have to him, we witness a great miracle. People are fed, and God is glorified.

1. *State of Food Insecurity in the World 2006*. Food and Agriculture Organization of the United Nations, 2006.

2. Jeffrey D. Sachs, "The End of Poverty," Time.com, March 6, 2005, http://www.time.com/time/magazine/article/0,9171,1034738,00.html (accessed October 1, 2007).

Abundant Bread
(Barley Wheat)

Welcome, children. I'm so glad you're here and we can share some bread together. I have another kind of bread for you to taste. *(pass out the bread)* This is barley bread. It's one of the oldest kinds of bread we know. It's easy to grow, but it doesn't always taste as good as wheat bread. That's why sometimes barley is called "poor people's" bread. Back in Bible times, rich people ate wheat bread and poor people ate barley bread. What do you think? Do you like it?

Tonight, we hear the story of a miracle that Jesus did. A huge crowd had gathered to hear Jesus speak. They wanted to learn what Jesus had to say about God. But after a long day the people were hungry. They didn't have any food. Where would they get enough bread to feed everyone? One little boy volunteered his supper. He had five loaves of barley bread and two fish (John 6:9). So Jesus took those loaves and fish and prayed over them. Then he started breaking the loaves and fish into pieces, and it says that he fed over 5,000 people. That's pretty amazing, isn't it, with only five loaves of bread and two fish? It says that everyone ate as much as they wanted, and there were leftovers!

I love this story because it tells us a lot about God. God isn't selfish or stingy. God loves us so much that God gives and gives and gives. That's what the word abundant means. God's love for us is abundant, more than we can count, more than we can even imagine. It is a bunch of love. God loves us so much that he gave us Jesus, the best gift ever.

Now I need your help again. Will you take this bread out to the congregation? I want you to be little preachers and when each person gets a piece of bread I want you to say, "God loves you a bunch."

Say that with me. *(let them repeat it a few times)* Thank you. Let us pray. We thank you God that you love us so abundantly. We thank you for giving us Jesus. Teach us how to share your blessings so that all the world might be fed. Amen.

Honey Barley Wheat Bread

Ingredients
1 1/2 teaspoons yeast
1 3/4 cups bread flour
1 1/4 cups whole wheat flour
1/2 cup barley flour
3 Tablespoons vital gluten
1/2 teaspoon salt
1/4 cup honey
1 1/2 cups water

Directions
Put all ingredients in the machine in the order they are given. Start the machine. If necessary, add additional water by the Tablespoon until a single ball of dough forms. Set on sweet, medium-dark setting.

Maundy Thursday
1 Corinthians 11:17-34

Body Bread

A few years ago, I participated in a World Hunger Meal. The point of the meal was to sensitize us to the reality of hunger in our world today. When people arrived at the meal, they were assigned to a group that represented a certain part of the world's population. Here's how we were divided up. The wealthiest 20% had 83% of the world's income. The next 20% lived on 12% of the world's income. The third 20% had a little more than 2%. The fourth 20% had a little below 2%. And the poorest 20% had just 1% of the world's income.[1] We began our meal sitting ten per table, each group being represented by two people. We had no idea which group we represented before the meal began. As the food arrived those in the first group received two turkey cutlets, cranberry rice, bread, a side salad, a choice of beverage, and dessert. The second group got a little less cranberry rice, a side salad, and a choice of beverage. The third group at the table got plain rice, a side salad, bread, and water. The fourth group got plain rice, a side salad, and water. Lastly, the poorest group received just plain rice and water. The food was brought to the table without any instructions. It was interesting to see how quickly people became uncomfortable with the situation. Those who represented the wealthiest group began to feel guilty at having so much and started to share with those who represented the poorest. Comments were made like, "That is so not fair!" or "That's so mean!" It was an effective way to visualize a reality of our world that we don't easily see. Today, 854 million people in our world are hungry. How are we as Christians to respond?[2]

Those comments at the Hunger Meal are a loose translation of the instructions the apostle Paul gave the church at Corinth. Paul was critical of the way they practiced holy communion. Apparently, the church had communion in the context of a meal. Some of the wealthier Christians were feasting while the poorer believers

61

went hungry. In verse 22 Paul said that behavior showed "contempt for the church" and also humiliated the poor. "In this matter I do not commend you."

But how could Paul motivate the Corinthians to change their practice? What kind of argument could he make? Paul took them back to the first Lord's Supper, back to the night Jesus was betrayed, the first Maundy Thursday (vv. 23-26). Then Paul told them that there was a right way and a wrong way to come to the Lord's Supper. "For all who eat and drink without discerning the body, eat and drink judgment against themselves" (v. 29). What did he mean "discerning the body"? It's clear from the context that Paul means the body of Christ in the community. In effect he is saying, recognize Christ in your fellow Christians. Treat each other with generosity and hospitality, just as you would treat Jesus. When we fail to do this, the community is weakened. Paul goes on to talk about the importance of each member of the community (ch. 12) and the importance of love in the community (ch. 13). Love shares generously with others the blessings God has given.

Holy communion was a serious affair in the church I grew up in. We had communion only once a month. At every communion service, the words of the apostle Paul were printed in the bulletin.

> Whoever, therefore, eats the bread or drinks the cup of the Lord in an unworthy manner will be answerable for the body and blood of the Lord. Examine yourselves, and only then eat of the bread and drink of the cup. For all who eat and drink without discerning the body, eat and drink judgment against themselves.
> — 1 Corinthians 11:27-29

Those verses scared me. Communion was serious business requiring a lot of introspection and preparation. If I had any doubts at all that I was participating in an unworthy manner I should just stay in my pew and forget communion or God was going to judge me. Many years later I have come to see things differently. Surely, it is important to have some understanding about communion and treat the sacrament with respect and reverence. But communion is not just about seeing Jesus in the bread. Communion is also seeing Jesus in the community, the body of Christ. Holy communion is personal, but it is never private. When we participate in the Lord's Supper without sensing the body of Christ in those around us, something is wrong. When we ignore the needs of others and refuse to share, there is a problem and our experience of communion is diminished.

"Because there is one bread, we who are many are one body, for we all partake of the one bread" (1 Corinthians 10:17). The hymn, "As The Grains Of Wheat," talks about how various grains of wheat from different parts of the field are all brought together to form one loaf of bread. That is the image of people from all over the world coming together in the one body of Christ.[3]

Have you ever baked bread from scratch? Think about what's involved. You likely bought the flour at the store, opened the bag and measured out what you needed. Most of us never see the mill where that flour is processed. Nor do we see the farmer harvesting the individual stalks of wheat. The next time you look at bread, whether store bought or baked yourself, I hope you look beneath the crust and see the one loaf as the contribution of many individual stalks of wheat. And the next time you eat bread at the Lord's table I hope you see in it the body of Christ, a coming together of Christ's family throughout the earth. I hope it reminds you that you are connected not only to Christ, but to his body, the church.

The apostle Paul criticized those who were rich, who came to holy communion while ignoring the hungry. He felt this made a mockery of the Eucharist. Discerning the body of Christ was impossible if one ignored the hungry. In his book, *Rich Christians in an Age of Hunger*, author Ron Sider puts it this way. "As long as any Christian anywhere in the world is hungry, the eucharistic celebration of all Christians everywhere in the world is imperfect."[4]

On this night when we remember that Christ has given us his body and blood to feed our deepest hunger, may we renew our commitment to see him in those around us, and to share our blessings with all who are hungry.

1. Ron Sider, *Rich Christians in an Age of Hunger: Moving From Affluence to Generosity* (Dallas: Word Publishers, 1997), pp. 2-3.

2. For more details on the Hunger Meal visit the ELCA World Hunger website at http.//www.elca.org/hunger/resources/youth.html.

3. "As The Grains Of Wheat" by Marty Haugen © 1990 GIA Publications. For various options available for the reprinting of this hymn, go to OneLicense@www.OneLicense.net.

4. *Op cit*, Ron Sider, pp. 85-86.

Pumpernickel Bread

Ingredients
1 cup plus 3 Tablespoons water
1/4 cup molasses
2 Tablespoons vegetable oil
1/2 cup whole wheat
1/2 cup rye flour
1/4 cup cornmeal
2 Tablespoons unsweetened cocoa
1 teaspoon instant coffee
2 1/2 cups bread flour
1 1/2 teaspoons salt
2 Tablespoons vital wheat gluten
2 teaspoons active dry yeast (about 1 1/2 teaspoon bread machine
    or rapid yeast)
2 teaspoons caraway seeds, optional

Directions
    Add ingredients to your bread machine according to manu-
facturer's suggested order. Use medium crust setting. Makes a 2-
pound loaf.

Sweet Potato Yeast Bread

Ingredients
1/2 cup plus 2 Tablespoons water
1 teaspoon vanilla extract
1 cup mashed sweet potatoes
4 cups bread flour
1/4 teaspoons each ground nutmeg and cinnamon
2 Tablespoons butter
1/3 cup dark brown sugar
1 1/2 teaspoons salt
2 teaspoons active dry yeast
2 Tablespoons dry milk

Directions

Add ingredients according to the manufacturer's suggested order. Use white bread setting, light crust. Makes a 2-pound loaf.

Betrayer's Bread

Good Friday is a story of betrayal. But who, exactly, betrayed Jesus that day?

Jesus shared a special meal with his disciples. It was holiday time — the Festival of Unleavened Bread. The disciples were unaware that this would be their last meal with Jesus. Special preparations were made. During the meal Jesus said something that completely changed the atmosphere. "Truly I tell you, one of you will betray me, one who is eating with me" (Mark 14:18). You can imagine the kind of impact a statement like that would have. To share a meal with someone in that culture was an expression of acceptance and intimacy. To be betrayed by someone in your inner circle was particularly offensive. Jesus and his disciples were reclining at the table, as was the custom back then. A loaf of bread was passed among them, each one breaking off a piece. Having no spoons or forks, the bread was dipped into a communal bowl filled with stew. But who was the betrayer?

> *They began to be distressed and to say to him one after another, "Surely, not I?" He said to them, "It is one of the twelve, one who is dipping bread into the bowl with me. For the Son of Man goes as it is written of him, but woe to that one by whom the Son of Man is betrayed! It would have been better for that one not to have been born."* — Mark 14:19-21

Even though Jesus knew that Judas was going to betray him, Jesus still extended him table fellowship. Jesus shared bread with Judas. But for Judas, this was no bread of fellowship; it was the bread of betrayal.

It wasn't only Judas who betrayed Jesus that day. Later, Jesus predicted that all the disciples would desert him, and even Peter himself would deny Jesus three times. In a sense they all deserted Jesus, denied him, betrayed him.

I love the words from the Lenten hymn, "Were You There?" — "Were you there when they crucified my Lord?" The question is rather poetic, and the answer, at first glance, is obvious. How could I have been at an event that happened 2,000 years ago? Yet the hymn writer wants us to look deeper. Are you sure you weren't there?

In the Old Testament the Jews had a confession of faith they were to make. In Deuteronomy, it says,

> *You shall make this response before the Lord your God: "A wandering Aramean was my ancestor; he went down into Egypt and lived there as an alien, few in number, and there he became a great nation, mighty and populous. When the Egyptians treated us harshly and afflicted us, by imposing hard labor on us, we cried to the Lord, the God of our ancestors; the Lord heard our voice and saw our affliction, our toil, and our oppression. The Lord brought us out of Egypt with a mighty hand and an outstretched arm, with a terrifying display of power, and with signs and wonders; and he brought us into this place and gave us this land, a land flowing with milk and honey."*
> — Deuteronomy 26:5-9

Now, let me read it again, but this time please give close attention to the pronouns. Notice the shift from third person singular "he" to first person plural "we." This confession of faith, about the central event of salvation in the Old Testament, is written in the historical present. It is not just ancient history, but the history of every Jew, past, present, and future. If asked the question, "Were you there?" when God delivered Israel from Egypt, every Jew would answer with a definitive, "Yes!"

That is exactly how the Bible presents the central act of salvation in the New Testament — the death and resurrection of Jesus Christ. It is not just ancient history; it is "ourstory." To answer the hymn writer's question, we *were* there when they crucified our Lord.

68

We were there when they nailed him to the tree and laid him in the tomb. And yes, we were there when he rose up from the grave. The apostle Paul tells us that in baptism we were joined to Christ's death and resurrection. Yes, we were there. Christ's story, is "ourstory"!

I have another favorite Lenten hymn — "Ah, Holy Jesus." The hymn writer asks the same question we began with: Who was it who betrayed Jesus?

> *Who was the guilty? Who brought this upon thee?*
> *Alas, my treason, Jesus, hath undone thee.*
> *'Twas I, Lord Jesus, I it was denied thee: I crucified*
> *thee.*[1]

We weren't just there at Jesus' death, passive spectators watching bad people do evil things to our Lord. We were the ones who betrayed and crucified him. We were the ones who arrested him, who mocked him, and spit in his face. We were the ones who whipped him and drove the nails into his hands and feet. It was my sin, your sin, which drove Jesus to the cross. You and I crucified Jesus.

So back to our original question — "Who betrayed Jesus?" It was not just Judas who betrayed Jesus. We were there, you and I. It was our sins that drove Jesus to the cross, our rebellion that drove the nails into his hands and feet. We are the betrayers eating betrayer's bread with our Lord.

This reminds me of another story of betrayal in the popular children's book, *The Lion, the Witch, and the Wardrobe* by C. S. Lewis. Four children — two brothers and two sisters — enter the magical land of Narnia. The other three, Peter, Lucy, and Susan, were unaware that Edmund had been there once before, had met the White Witch, and had eaten her enchanted Turkish Delight. Caught in the Witch's snare, Edmund betrayed his brother and sisters to the White Witch. Eventually he was rescued from the Witch's grasp by the followers of Aslan, the great Lion. But the White Witch showed up at Aslan's camp demanding her rights.

"You have a traitor there, Aslan," said the Witch. Of course everyone present knew that she meant Edmund....

"Well," said Aslan. "His offense was not against you."

"Have you forgotten the Deep Magic?" asked the Witch.

"Let us say I have forgotten it," answered Aslan gravely. "Tell us of this Deep Magic."

"Tell you?" said the Witch, her voice growing suddenly shriller. "Tell you what is written on the very Table of Stone which stands beside us? ... You at least know the magic which the Emperor put into Narnia at the very beginning. You know that every traitor belongs to me as my lawful prey and that for every treachery I have a right to a kill ... That human creature is mine. His life is forfeit to me. His blood is my property."

"Come and take it then," said the Bull with the man's head in a great bellowing voice.

"Fool," said the Witch with a savage smile that was almost a snarl, "do you really think your master can rob me of my rights by mere force? He knows the Deep Magic better than that. He knows that unless I have blood as the Law says all Narnia will be overturned and perish in fire and water."

"It is very true," said Aslan; "I do not deny it."[2]

The White Witch knew the deep magic quite well. Betrayal was a crime that demanded punishment. But Aslan offered her a trade. Instead of Edmund, Aslan would surrender himself. The Witch gladly accepted the offer, and in a heartbreaking scene, she puts Aslan to death. What the Witch didn't know, though, was that there was a deeper magic from before the dawn of time. It said, "When a willing victim who had committed no treachery was killed in a traitor's stead, the Table would crack and death itself would start working backward."[3] That is indeed what happened. The Table representing the deep magic cracked, and Aslan was raised from the dead. The demands of the deep magic on Edmund's life were satisfied, and he was released from his guilt.

Edmund's story is our story. Judas' story is our story. Jesus gave himself for us on the cross. "But God proves his love for us in that while we still were sinners Christ died for us" (Romans 5:8). If Good Friday is a story of betrayal, it is also a story of forgiveness. Betrayer's bread was eaten, but also another bread. "While they were eating, he took a loaf of bread, and after blessing it he broke it, gave it to them, and said, 'Take; this is my body' " (Mark 14:22). Jesus gives his body even to traitors. It is the bread of life for the forgiveness of sin. That is the good news in Good Friday. Thanks be to God.

----

1. "Ah, Holy Jesus" by Johann Heermann. The hymn is in the public domain.

2. C. S. Lewis, *The Lion, the Witch, and the Wardrobe* (New York: Harper Collins Publishers, 1994), p. 141.

3. *Ibid*, p. 162.

Herb Bread

Ingredients
1 cup warm water
1 beaten egg
1 teaspoon salt
2 Tablespoons sugar
2 Tablespoons olive oil
2 teaspoons dried rosemary or use 2 Tablespoons fresh, crumbled
1 teaspoon each dried oregano and basil (or 1 Tablespoon each fresh)
3 cups flour
2 teaspoons bread machine yeast

Directions
Place in machine according to machine instructions (or if you make bread by hand, you already know what to do). A few minutes into kneading, check that the dough is the consistency that you want, add any flour or extra water that you need (I usually find I need a little bit more flour).

Bake on large loaf, with a light crust setting. This herb combination smells heavenly. You can use any combination of herbs you like, and adjust it to complement whatever you are serving with it.

Kalamata Olive Bread

Ingredients
1/3 to 1/2 cup brine from olives
Warm water, enough to make 1 1/2 cups when combined with brine
2 Tablespoons olive oil
3 cups bread flour
1 2/3 cups whole wheat flour
1 1/2 teaspoons salt
2 Tablespoons sugar
1 1/2 teaspoons dried leaf basil
2 teaspoons active dry yeast
1/2 to 2/3 cup finely chopped kalamata olives (about 2 dozen pitted olives)

Directions
Put brine in a 2-cup measure; add warm water to make 1 1/2 cups. Put all ingredients, except for the olives, in the bread machine according to your manufacturer's preferred order. Choose basic or wheat setting; add olives at the beep.

The Bread Of Life

Christ is risen! He is risen indeed! Jesus said, "I am the bread of life ... I am the living bread that came down from heaven. Whoever eats of this bread will live forever ..." (John 6:48-51). Brothers and sisters in Christ — grace to you and peace from God our Father and our risen Lord and Savior Jesus the Christ. Amen.

Bread is called the staff of life. It is the staff we lean on for our journey from birth to death. Bread has been the staff we have leaned on this past Lent. This Easter morning, we end our journey with the Bread of Life.

Many of you will enjoy a special meal today. Holiday meals are good times to gather the family together. We want them to be wonderful. We may look to Martha Stewart on ideas for decorating. We may ask Emeril Lagasse to help us "kick it up a notch" in the kitchen. Or, perhaps we'll go out and let others do the cooking. We will stuff ourselves and compliment the cooks on how wonderful everything is. But tomorrow we will get hungry again. There will be more meals to fix and more bread to eat in order to keep body and soul together. That's one way to look at life — an endless parade of meals.

Have you ever stood at a grave and hoped that there was more to life? Somehow, when faced with death, many of the things that give meaning to our lives just don't seem to be enough. Eating, sleeping, learning and working, loving and being loved, as important as these are, we human beings seem to want and need more lasting meaning for our lives. If this life is all there is, then we might as well "eat, drink, and be merry for tomorrow we die." The good news is that there is more to life. On this Easter Sunday Jesus offers us the bread of life "so that one may eat of it and not die." Christ is risen. Death is defeated. We are given a food that sustains us in this world and the next.

Did you know that food is an important part of how the Bible portrays heaven? Heaven is like a banquet, a wedding feast. The Old Testament prophet Isaiah painted a vivid picture of heaven.

> *On this mountain the Lord of hosts will make for all*
> *peoples a feast of rich food, a feast of well-aged wines,*
> *of rich food filled with marrow, of well-aged wines*
> *strained clear. And he will destroy on this mountain the*
> *shroud that is cast over all peoples, the sheet that is*
> *spread over all nations; he will swallow up death for-*
> *ever. Then the Lord God will wipe away the tears from*
> *all faces, and the disgrace of his people he will take*
> *away from all the earth, for the Lord has spoken.*
> — Isaiah 25:6-8

The greatest chefs in the world couldn't come close to this feast. Rich food and well-aged wine God promises to all people. That is what God feeds us. But did you notice what God eats? "God will swallow up death forever." God eats death; we eat eternal life.

I wonder if the apostle Paul had this in mind when he wrote about the resurrection to the church at Corinth. "When this perishable body puts on imperishability, and this mortal body puts on immortality, then the saying that is written will be fulfilled: 'Death has been swallowed up in victory' " (1 Corinthians 15:54). How are we to think of the death and resurrection of Jesus Christ? Jesus has eaten death, tasted it fully, and swallowed it completely. His resurrection proves that death is defeated. Christ is the victor. He has eaten what we could not. And we are now offered the bread of life "so that one may eat of it and not die."

There is a story of a frugal man from Scotland who came to America many years ago. He had purchased passage on one of the great ocean liners. Not having any money, he decided to save on food by stocking up on crackers, cheese, and fruit before he left. The ship sailed, and he began to eat his skimpy meals. This went fairly well for the first four or five days. But as the ship drew closer to New York the crackers got stale, the cheese became moldy, and the fruit spoiled. Finally, there was nothing left that was fit to eat. The man decided that he would go to the dining room and have one good meal before the ship docked and he went ashore. Imagine his surprise to discover that nothing in the dining room cost anything, and that all that he could ever have eaten had already been included in the price of his ticket!

Today, Jesus is offering us the bread of life. It's free, paid for on the cross. Grab hold of it, taste it, and savor this life-giving food that nourishes the deepest part of our souls.

Several years ago, a man wrote a letter to the editor of a newspaper. He said he couldn't remember any sermons preached in church and he questioned whether they were all that important. "I have been attending a church service for the past thirty years and have heard probably 3,000 sermons," he wrote. "To my consternation I discovered that I cannot remember a single one!" Many readers responded in the Letters to the Editor column, but this letter settled the issue: "I have been married thirty years. During that time I have eaten 32,850 meals — mostly of my wife's cooking. Suddenly, I have discovered that I cannot remember the menu of a single meal. And yet, I received nourishment from every single one of them. I have the distinct impression that without them, I would have starved to death long ago." I suspect many of us are like that man. We don't remember many of the sermons we have heard. But what we do know is that somehow God's Spirit gave us exactly what we needed to hear, and we were fed and nourished. We were given the bread of life.

Today is Easter. We celebrate the resurrection of our Lord and his victory over death. We acknowledge that the power of death is all too real. We see it in our world in wars, hunger, poverty, and disease. We see it in our homes when families fight and hurt each other. We see it in ourselves when we give in to temptations we know are wrong. But today we are here to claim the victory won by Jesus Christ. Today, we celebrate a power that is stronger than death. Jesus Christ is able to enter the most hopeless situations and transform them. That is the message of Easter. Death has been swallowed up and transformed by the power of God. That is the resurrection! And today we are given a foretaste of the resurrection feast that will be ours in heaven. "I am the bread of life," Jesus said. "I am the living bread that came down from heaven. Whoever eats of this bread will live forever" (John 6:51). People of God, today is Easter. Today you have eternal life. You have the power of Christ's resurrection in you to turn whatever of death's power you are dealing with into new life. Today, let us eat the bread of life and join our voices in praising God. Alleluia! Alleluia! Alleluia!

Favorite Morning Bread

Ingredients
2 teaspoons active dry yeast
2 1/2 cups bread flour
1/2 cup whole wheat flour
1 Tablespoon instant coffee (mix coffee in with water)
1 teaspoon cinnamon
1 teaspoon salt
2 Tablespoons nonfat dry milk
1 Tablespoon oil/butter
1/4 cup honey
1 1/4 cups warm water

Directions
Add ingredients according to the manufacturer's directions for your bread machine.

Granary Bread

Ingredients
1/4 cup cracked wheat
2 Tablespoons millet
1 cup boiling water
1 1/4 cups water
2 Tablespoons molasses or honey
2 teaspoons shortening
2 cups whole wheat flour
1 cup bread flour
1/4 cup regular or quick-cooking rolled oats
3 Tablespoons cornmeal
2 Tablespoons toasted wheat germ or unprocessed wheat bran
1 Tablespoon gluten flour
3/4 teaspoon salt
1 teaspoon active dry yeast or bread machine yeast

Directions
In a small bowl, combine the cracked wheat and millet. Add the 1 cup boiling water. Let stand for five minutes; drain well.

Add the remaining ingredients to a 1 1/2- to 2-pound bread machine, according to the manufacturer's directions, adding the cracked wheat mixture with the water. If available, select the whole grain cycle or select the basic white bread cycle, and desired crust setting. Makes one 1 1/2-pound loaf (16 servings).

Sweet Oatmeal Bread

Ingredients
3/4 cup old-fashioned rolled oats
1 1/4 to 1 3/8 cups water
3 Tablespoons molasses
1 1/2 Tablespoons sugar
1 1/2 teaspoons salt
3 cups bread flour
1 1/2 teaspoons active dry yeast

Directions
Place all ingredients in 1 1/2-pound (medium) bread pan, using the least amount of liquid listed in the recipe. Select light crust setting. Press start.

Observe the dough as it kneads. After five to ten minutes, if it appears dry and stiff or if your machine sounds as if it's straining to knead it, add more liquid 1 Tablespoon at a time until the dough forms a smooth, soft, pliable ball that is slightly tacky to the touch. Use the light crust, standard bake cycle. Optional bake settings are whole wheat, sweet bread, delayed timer, or rapid bake.

After the baking cycle ends, remove bread from the pan, place the loaf on a cake rack, and allow to cool for one hour before slicing.

Cake Bread

Ingredients
1 cup water or milk
2 Tablespoons butter or oleo
1 cup cake mix, any flavor
2 1/2 cups bread flour
2 teaspoons yeast
1/8 to 1/4 teaspoon vanilla
1 to 3 Tablespoons poppy seeds

Directions
    Put all ingredients in the bread machine according to machine directions. Bake on basic setting. Makes a 2-pound loaf.

Whole Wheat Raisin Nut Cinnamon Bread

Ingredients
1 1/2 teaspoons yeast
2 cups whole wheat flour
2 cups white bread flour
1 1/2 teaspoon salt
1 1/2 teaspoon cinnamon
1 Tablespoon sugar
1 Tablespoon brown sugar
2 Tablespoons dry milk
2 Tablespoons butter
1 1/4 cups plus 2 Tablespoons warm water

Directions
Add ingredients according to the order listed. Five minutes before the end of the second kneading (some machines have a bell at that time), add the following:

1/2 cup raisins
1/2 cup chopped walnuts

www.ingramcontent.com/pod-product-compliance
Lightning Source LLC
Chambersburg PA
CBHW071018040426
42443CB00007B/833